# Breaking the Big Words
## A Syllable Division Activity Series

# Volume 2
## Syllable Pattern: V/CV
## Syllable Types: Cl, Op, ME, VP, BR, C-le

Josh Morgan, M.A. Ed.

Literacy Specialist
Special Educator
Intervention Coach

# Breaking the Big Words
## Volume 2: V/CV
# Table of Contents

# What is
# Breaking the Big Words?

## Introduction & Overview

The "Breaking the Big Words" Syllabication Activity Series provides scaffolded, research-based instruction on dividing syllables, identifying syllable types, and generalizing the skills to decode words and sentences.

This is the second Volume of the series and focuses on V/CV syllable pattern. There are six activity sets with each successive set introducing a new syllable type. With each set a new syllable type is added to build up to three-syllable words containing any of the six syllable types. Volume three introduces the VC/V syllable pattern.

Each set includes strategies for navigating consonant blends and digraphs when dividing syllables with visual supports to prompt students on Versions A and B. These prompts are faded on Version C to ensure students do not become dependent on the prompts. Anchor words are used as a visual support on Versions A and B of the activity sheets to remind students of strategies and the placement of each label. These visuals are faded on Version C. The same anchor words used on the activity sheets are provided as posters for classroom display to reference while reading, spelling, or writing unfamiliar words that may adhere to the syllable pattern.

To ensure skill generalization to basic reading, on the same activity sheet, students break words (slash between syllables) BEFORE reading a word list then WHILE reading sentences. Sight words are controlled in the series and consist primarily of PrePrimer and Primer Dolch words.

Each Activity Set of "Breaking the Big Words" employs three levels of scaffolding, embedded differentiation, a strong visual component, developmentally appropriate activities, and an instructional framework (Scope and Sequence).

# Find me on the web!

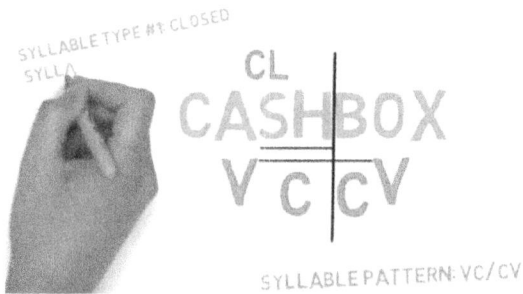

Companion videos for
Breaking the Big Words
can be found on my YouTube channel
www.youtube.com/c/JMorgan

Be sure to stop by my TPT store

for the first three parts of SOS to Encode! An Intensive Multisensory Reading, Writing, and Spelling Program.

TPT: Mr. Morgan's Multisensory for Teachers and Coaches

Paperback and Kindle versions of SOS to Encode! Parts 1, 2, & 3 are now available on Amazon

To download a free supplement to all parts of SOS to Encode!
joshmorganconsulting.com/freedownloads

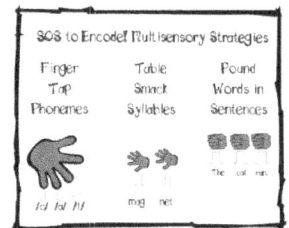

Subscribe to my to my email list to receive bonus content, receive a free product today, and test new products for free.

joshmorganconsulting.com/subscribe

# Features of
# Breaking the Big Words

## Research Based Strategies

- Syllabication: Consistent, systematic procedure for dividing multisyllabic words.
- Syllable Types: Students use a mnemonic device to recall, label, determine vowel sound, and decode syllable types.
- Long and Short Vowels: Labeling and decoding of syllables with long and short vowels.
- Decoding:
  - The last step of syllabication is always to decode the word.
  - Students decode in multiple contexts following syllabication for generalization.

## Scaffolding:

- Multiple visual supports are employed to differentiate the activities. This ensures each student is able to work at their level and fosters independence, confidence, and success with the strategy.
- As students gain skills, supports are gradually removed to promote independence.

## Components of each activity:

- New Words: Introduced during this activity.
- Review: Familiar syllable types and patterns for practice and maintenance.
- Break before You Read (word list): This step, following syllabication, uses the informal, "break" strategy. Students insert a slash to separate syllables. This occurs prior to reading the words.
- Break While You Read: This activity continues the generalization as students use the "break" strategy. Students read two sentences and "break" words as they come to them.

# Beyond BTBW

## Add additional levels of generalization

- As students progress through the activity sets incorporate supplemental activities that require students to divide syllables with known syllable types and patterns.

- For example, once students are able to divide words with closed syllables and VC/CV pattern, you can use these words with:
  - Spelling Words by asking the students to...
    - Write spelling words and "Break Before You Read."
    - Write sentences or stories with the words then divide them.
    - Read spelling sentences or stories written by peers and "Break While You Read."

  - Vocabulary Words by asking students to...
    - Break math, science, and social studies vocabulary words before beginning a new unit or chapter.
    - Read a historical text or article and "Break While You Read."
    - Break difficult words in math word problems to help students decode and understand the task.

  - Decodable Passages, Books and Stories by asking to:
    - Find difficult words and "Break Before You Read."
    - "Break While You Read" then reflect with a small group.

  - Tests, Worksheets, & Directions by asking students to...
    - Break words in directions to improve understanding,
    - "Break While You Read" on tests and worksheets to generalize skills to assessments.

# Scope & Sequence

- This is Volume 2 and the "Blue Set" of activities. Each set will focus on a single syllable pattern and will progress to cover each of the six syllable types within that pattern.
- Syllable patterns are introduced in a specific order to ensure students master a single syllable type with blends and digraphs before moving on to the next type.
- As students reach mastery with recognizing and decoding each syllable type, the next will be introduced.

# Full Series

| Volume | Color | Syllable Pattern | Syllable Types |
|--------|-------|------------------|----------------|
| 1 | Red | VC/CV | Cl, Op, ME, VP, BR, C-le |
| 2 | Blue | V/CV | Cl, Op, ME, VP, BR, C-le |
| 3 | Green | VC/V | Cl, Op, ME, VP, BR |
| 4 | Orange | V/V | Cl, Op, ME, VP, BR |

# Volume 2 Sets 8 to 13

| Set | Syllable Pattern | Syllable Types |
|-----|------------------|----------------|
| 8 | V/CV | Closed & Open |
| 9 | V/CV | Open & Closed |
| 10 | V/CV | Magic E, Op, & Cl |
| 11 | V/CV | Vowel Pairs, ME, Op, & Cl |
| 12 | V/CV | Bossy R, VP, ME, Op, & Cl |
| 13 | V/CV | Consonant-le, BR, VP, ME, Op, & Cl |

# Common Core State Standards

## Print Concepts

**K**
RF.K.1 Demonstrate understanding of the organization and basic features of print.
RF.K.1a Follow words from left to right, top to bottom, and page by page.
RF.K.1b Recognize that spoken words are represented in written language by specific sequences of letters.
RF.K.1c Understand that words are separated by spaces in print.

**1**
RF.1.1 Demonstrate understanding of the organization and basic features of print.
RF.1.1a Recognize the distinguishing features of a sentence (e.g., first word, capitalization, ending punctuation).

## Phonological Awareness

**K**
RF.K.2 Demonstrate understanding of spoken words, syllables, and sounds (phonemes).
RF.K.2b Count, pronounce, blend, and segment syllables in spoken words.
RF.K.2c Blend and segment onsets and rimes of single-syllable spoken words.

**1**
RF.1.2 Demonstrate understanding of spoken words, syllables, and sounds (phonemes).
RF.1.2a Distinguish long from short vowel sounds in spoken single-syllable words.
RF.1.2b Orally produce single-syllable words by blending sounds (phonemes), including consonant blends.
RF.1.2c Isolate and pronounce initial, medial vowel, and final sounds (phonemes) in spoken single-syllable words.
RF.1.2d Segment spoken single-syllable words into their complete sequence of individual sounds (phonemes).

## Phonics and Word Recognition

**K**
RF.K.3 Know and apply grade-level phonics and word analysis skills in decoding words.
RF.K.3a Demonstrate basic knowledge of one-to-one letter-sound correspondences by producing the primary sound or many of the most frequent sounds for each consonant.
RF.K.3b Associate the long and short sounds with the common spellings (graphemes) for the five major vowels.
RF.K.3c Read common high-frequency words by sight (e.g., the, of, to, you, she, my, is, are, do, does).

**1**
RF.1.3 Know and apply grade-level phonics and word analysis skills in decoding words.
RF.1.3a Know the spelling-sound correspondences for common consonant digraphs.
RF.1.3b Decode regularly spelled one-syllable words.
RF.1.3c Know final -e and common vowel team conventions for representing long vowel sounds.
RF.1.3d Use knowledge that every syllable must have a vowel sound to determine the number of syllables in a printed word.
RF.1.3e Decode two-syllable words following basic patterns by breaking the words into syllables.
RF.1.3g Recognize and read grade-appropriate irregularly spelled words.

**2**
RF.2.3 Know and apply grade-level phonics and word analysis skills in decoding words.
RF.2.3a Distinguish long and short vowels when reading regularly spelled one-syllable words.
RF.2.3b Know spelling-sound correspondences for additional common vowel teams.
RF.2.3c Decode regularly spelled two-syllable words with long vowels.
RF.2.3d Decode words with common prefixes and suffixes.
RF.2.3e Identify words with inconsistent but common spelling-sound correspondences.
RF.2.3f Recognize and read grade-appropriate irregularly spelled words.

**3**
RF.3.3 Know and apply grade-level phonics and word analysis skills in decoding words.
RF.3.3a Identify and know the meaning of the most common prefixes and derivational suffixes.
RF.3.3b Decode words with common Latin suffixes.
RF.3.3c Decode multi-syllable words.
RF.3.3d Read grade-appropriate irregularly spelled words.

| Fluency | |
|---|---|
| K | RF.K.4 Read emergent-reader texts with purpose and understanding. |
| 1 | RF.1.4 Read with sufficient accuracy and fluency to support comprehension. |
| 2 | RF.2.4 Read with sufficient accuracy and fluency to support comprehension.<br>RF.2.4a Read grade-level text with purpose and understanding.<br>RF.2.4b Read grade-level text orally with accuracy, appropriate rate, and expression on successive readings.<br>RF.2.4c<br>Use context to confirm or self-correct word recognition and understanding, rereading as necessary. |
| 3 | RF.3.4 Read with sufficient accuracy and fluency to support comprehension.<br>RF.3.4a  Read grade-level text with purpose and understanding.<br>RF.3.4c Use context to confirm or self-correct word recognition and understanding, rereading as necessary. |

# Visual Supports & Scaffolding

Each Activity has three levels or versions.
Level A activities provide highest level of visual supports while Level C provides the least.

| Supports | Version | | |
|---|---|---|---|
| | A | B | C |
| Steps for Dividing Syllables | YES | YES | YES |
| Visual Model with Bridge | YES | YES | NO |
| Consonant blends/digraphs underlined | YES | YES | NO |
| Models for Breaking Before and While Reading | YES | YES | NO |
| Boxes to guide syllable division | YES | NO | NO |

# Suggested Implementation Options

*There are many ways to use this resource. Below are two suggestions with additional details.*

Option 1:
- Activities can be distributed to a class or group of students based on their ability to complete the work independently.
  - Students who struggle more would get the version with the most supports while others can get a version with less supports.
  - While pre-teaching or reviewing, all students will have the same words and will be able to follow along with the lesson while using sheets with different levels of support.

Option 2:
- Teacher uses all three versions/levels with all students each week to scaffold the entire group together (small or whole group).
  - Students would all have same version of the activity at the same time.
  - During the week, the teacher begins with Version A (most support) and decreases support until students can complete Version C (least support) before moving on.
  - This option is great for small groups and intervention groups with students struggling to read and write multisyllabic words.

# Activity Set 8

## Syllable Type Focus: Closed

### Scope and Sequence

| Activity Number | Syllable Pattern | 1st Syllable Type | 2nd Syllable Type | 3rd Syllable Type | Phonics |
|---|---|---|---|---|---|
| 1 | V/CV | Op | Cl | X | Single Phonemes |
| 2 | V/CV | Op | Cl | X | Blends |
| 3 | V/CV | Op | Cl | X | Blends & Digraphs |
| 4 | V/CV | Cl | Cl or Op | Cl | Single Phonemes |
| 5 | V/CV | Cl or Op | Cl or Op | Cl | Blends & Digraphs |

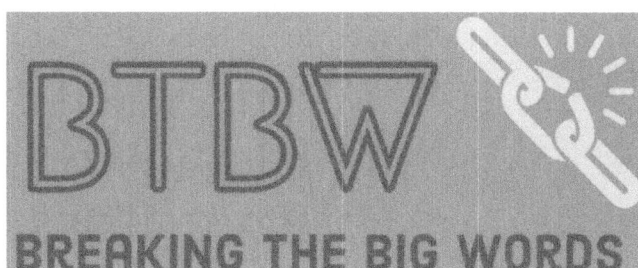

BTBW

**BREAKING THE BIG WORDS**

Follow the steps to divide the syllables.

1. Label the first two vowels.
2. Draw the bridge.
3. Label consonants on the bridge.
4. Choose pattern and break the word.
5. Repeat for any other syllables.
6. Label the syllable.

op    cl
**open**
V C V

New Words

Logan

pilot

Salem

open

basic

bonus

Break BEFORE you read

Lo/gan
pilot
Salem
open
basic
bonus

Break WHILE you read

Lo/gan could hear the thunder and went to speak with the pilot.

The pilot got on the plane to transport the inventors to Salem.

Name: _____

Activity 8.1    Version: B

op        cl

# open

V | C  V

## Follow the steps to divide the syllables.
1. Label the first two vowels.
2. Draw the bridge.
3. Label consonants on the bridge.
4. Choose pattern and break the word.
5. Repeat for any other syllables.
6. Label the syllable.

New Words

Logan

open

pilot

basic

Salem

bonus

Break BEFORE you read

Lo/gan
pilot
Salem
open
basic
bonus

Break WHILE you read

Lo/gan could hear the thunder and went to speak with the pilot.

The pilot got on the plane to transport the inventors to Salem.

13

<u>Follow the steps to divide the syllables.</u>
1. Label the first two vowels.
2. Draw the bridge.
3. Label consonants on the bridge.
4. Choose pattern and break the word.
5. Repeat for any other syllables.
6. Label the syllable.

New
Words

Logan

open

pilot

basic

Salem

bonus

Break BEFORE you read

Logan
pilot
Salem
open
basic
bonus

Break WHILE you read

Logan could hear the thunder and went to speak with the pilot.

The pilot got on the plane to transport the inventors to Salem.

Follow the steps to divide the syllables.
1. Label the first two vowels.
2. Draw the bridge.
3. Label consonants on the bridge.
4. Choose pattern and break the word.
5. Repeat for any other syllables.
6. Label the syllable.

op | cl
student
V | C V

New Words

student

silent

Review

unit

stupid

rodent

bison

Break BEFORE you read

stu/dent
silent
stupid
rodent
unit
bison

Break WHILE you read

The stu/dents had to stay silent during the unit test.

The merchant felt stupid after spending too much cash on the rodent.

Name: _____

Activity 8.2    Version: B

Follow the steps to divide the syllables.
1. Label the first two vowels.
2. Draw the bridge.
3. Label consonants on the bridge.
4. Choose pattern and break the word.
5. Repeat for any other syllables.
6. Label the syllable.

op    cl
s t u d e n t
V   C  V

student          stupid

New
Words

silent           rodent

Review

unit             bison

Break BEFORE you read

stu/dent
silent
stupid
rodent
unit
bison

Break WHILE you read

The stu/dents had to stay silent during the unit test.

The merchant felt stupid after spending too much cash on the rodent.

16

## Follow the steps to divide the syllables.
1. Label the first two vowels.
2. Draw the bridge.
3. Label consonants on the bridge.
4. Choose pattern and break the word.
5. Repeat for any other syllables.
6. Label the syllable.

New
Words

student          stupid

silent          rodent

Review

unit          bison

Break BEFORE you read

student
silent
stupid
rodent
unit
bison

Break WHILE you read

The students had to stay silent during the unit test.

The merchant felt stupid after spending too much cash on the rodent.

Follow the steps to divide the syllables.
1. Label the first two vowels.
2. Draw the bridge.
3. Label consonants on the bridge.
4. Choose pattern and break the word.
5. Repeat for any other syllables.
6. Label the syllable.

op | cl
r e c e s s
V | C V

New Words

thesis

recess

python

Irish

Review

locust

latent

Break BEFORE you read

the/sis
python
recess
Irish
locust
latent

Break WHILE you read

The facts in her es/say did support the central thesis.

The students ran when they saw the python at recess.

Follow the steps to divide the syllables.
1. Label the first two vowels.
2. Draw the bridge.
3. Label consonants on the bridge.
4. Choose pattern and break the word.
5. Repeat for any other syllables.
6. Label the syllable.

op    cl

r e c e s s

V | C V

New
Words

thesis

recess

python

Irish

Review

locust

latent

Break BEFORE you read

the/sis
python
recess
Irish
locust
latent

Break WHILE you read

The facts in her es/say did support the central thesis.

The students ran when they saw the python at recess.

Follow the steps to divide the syllables.
1. Label the first two vowels.
2. Draw the bridge.
3. Label consonants on the bridge.
4. Choose pattern and break the word.
5. Repeat for any other syllables.
6. Label the syllable.

New Words

thesis            recess

python            Irish

Review

locust            latent

Break BEFORE you read

thesis
python
recess
Irish
locust
latent

Break WHILE you read

The facts in her essay did support the central thesis.

The students ran when they saw the python at recess.

Follow the steps to divide the syllables.
1. Label the first two vowels.
2. Draw the bridge.
3. Label consonants on the bridge.
4. Choose pattern and break the word.
5. Repeat for any other syllables.
6. Label the syllable.

op | cl | cl
**gigan|tic**
V|C V|C C|V

## New Words

☐ ☐ ☐
gigantic
☐☐☐☐☐

☐ ☐ ☐
octopus
☐☐☐☐☐

☐ ☐ ☐
acrobat
☐☐☐☐☐

## Review

☐ ☐
climax
☐☐☐☐☐

☐ ☐
platform
☐☐☐☐☐

☐ ☐
omit
☐☐☐☐☐

Break BEFORE you read
gi/gan/tic
octopus
acrobat
climax
platform
omit

Break WHILE you read
We did not get to see the gi/gan/tic octopus in the lake.

At the climax, the acrobat did five back flips from the top of the platform.

Follow the steps to divide the syllables.
1. Label the first two vowels.
2. Draw the bridge.
3. Label consonants on the bridge.
4. Choose pattern and break the word.
5. Repeat for any other syllables.
6. Label the syllable.

op | cl | cl

gi|gan|tic

VCVCCV

## New Words

gigantic

octopus

acrobat

## Review

climax

platform

omit

Break BEFORE you read

gi/gan/tic
octopus
acrobat
climax
platform
omit

Break WHILE you read

We did not get to see the gi/gan/tic octopus in the lake.

At the climax, the acrobat did five back flips from the top of the platform.

Follow the steps to divide the syllables.
1. Label the first two vowels.
2. Draw the bridge.
3. Label consonants on the bridge.
4. Choose pattern and break the word.
5. Repeat for any other syllables.
6. Label the syllable.

New Words

Review

gigantic

climax

octopus

platform

acrobat

omit

Break BEFORE you read

gigantic
octopus
acrobat
climax
platform
omit

Break WHILE you read
We did not get to see the gigantic octopus in the lake.

At the climax, the acrobat did five back flips from the top of the platform.

Name: _____

## Follow the steps to divide the syllables.

1. Label the first two vowels.
2. Draw the bridge.
3. Label consonants on the bridge.
4. Choose pattern and break the word.
5. Repeat for any other syllables.
6. Label the syllable.

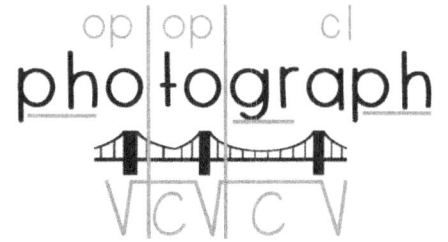

op | op | cl

## pho to graph

V | C V | C V

## New Words

☐  ☐        ☐

photograph

☐   ☐   ☐

innocent

☐   ☐   ☐

instrument

## Review

☐   ☐

bogus

☐   ☐

evil

☐   ☐

hotel

## Break BEFORE you read

pho/to/graph
innocent
instrument
bogus
evil
hotel

## Break WHILE you read

The pho/to/graph did show the students were innocent.

Do you still have a photograph of your first instrument?

Name: _____

Follow the steps to divide the syllables.
1. Label the first two vowels.
2. Draw the bridge.
3. Label consonants on the bridge.
4. Choose pattern and break the word.
5. Repeat for any other syllables.
6. Label the syllable.

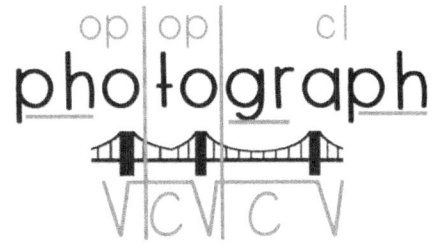

op | op        cl
pho|tograph
VCV C V

## New Words

photograph

innocent

instrument

## Review

bogus

evil

hotel

## Break BEFORE you read

pho/to/graph
innocent
instrument
bogus
evil
hotel

## Break WHILE you read

The pho/to/graph did show the students were innocent.

Do you still have a photograph of your first instrument?

Follow the steps to divide the syllables.
1. Label the first two vowels.
2. Draw the bridge.
3. Label consonants on the bridge.
4. Choose pattern and break the word.
5. Repeat for any other syllables.
6. Label the syllable.

New Words                                    Review

photograph                          bogus

innocent                            evil

instrument                          hotel

Break BEFORE you read          Break WHILE you read

photograph                     The photograph did show
innocent                       the students were
instrument                     innocent.
bogus
evil                           Do you still have a
hotel                          photograph of your first
                               instrument?

# Activity Set 9

# Syllable Type Focus: Open
## Scope and Sequence

| Activity Number | Syllable Pattern | 1st Syllable Type | 2nd Syllable Type | 3rd Syllable Type | Phonics |
|---|---|---|---|---|---|
| 1 | V/CV | Op | Op | X | Single Phonemes |
| 2 | V/CV | Op | Op | X | Blends |
| 3 | V/CV | Op | Op | X | Blends & Digraphs |
| 4 | V/CV | Op | Op | Cl | Single Phonemes |
| 5 | V/CV | Op | Op | Cl | Blends & Digraphs |

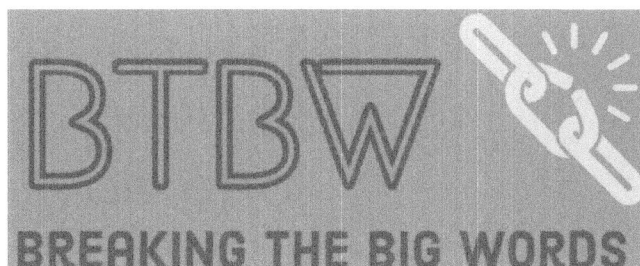

BTBW
**BREAKING THE BIG WORDS**

Name: _____

Activity 9.1    Version: A

## Follow the steps to divide the syllables.
1. Label the first two vowels.
2. Draw the bridge.
3. Label consonants on the bridge.
4. Choose pattern and break the word.
5. Repeat for any other syllables.
6. Label the syllable.

he|ro
op    op
V C V

New Words

hero

Cody

tiny

pony

cozy

logo

Break BEFORE you read

he/ro
Cody
tiny
pony
cozy
logo

Break WHILE you read

The he/ro set off to save Cody from the python.

The tiny pony went to his cozy spot after a long day.

Follow the steps to divide the syllables.
1. Label the first two vowels.
2. Draw the bridge.
3. Label consonants on the bridge.
4. Choose pattern and break the word.
5. Repeat for any other syllables.
6. Label the syllable.

h e r o

New
Words

hero                    Cody

tiny                    pony

cozy                    logo

Break BEFORE you read          Break WHILE you read

he/ro                          The he/ro set off to
Cody                           save Cody from the
tiny                           python.
pony
cozy                           The tiny pony went to
logo                           his cozy spot after a
                               long day.

Follow the steps to divide the syllables.
1. Label the first two vowels.
2. Draw the bridge.
3. Label consonants on the bridge.
4. Choose pattern and break the word.
5. Repeat for any other syllables.
6. Label the syllable.

New
Words

hero                          Cody

tiny                          pony

cozy                          logo

Break BEFORE you read        Break WHILE you read

hero                          The hero set off to
Cody                         save Cody from the
tiny                          python.
pony
cozy                         The tiny pony went to
logo                         his cozy spot after a
                             long day.

## Follow the steps to divide the syllables.
1. Label the first two vowels.
2. Draw the bridge.
3. Label consonants on the bridge.
4. Choose pattern and break the word.
5. Repeat for any other syllables.
6. Label the syllable.

op   op

g r a v y

V C V

New Words

☐ ☐
g r a v y
☐

☐ ☐
B r o d y
☐

☐ ☐
s l y l y
☐

☐ ☐
c r a z y
☐

Review

☐ ☐
l a z y
☐

☐ ☐
v e t o
☐

**Break BEFORE you read**

gra/vy
Brody
slyly
crazy
lazy
veto

**Break WHILE you read**

Bro/dy let the students in class play his game.

The rancher slyly snuck up on the bison.

Name: _____

**Follow the steps to divide the syllables.**
1. Label the first two vowels.
2. Draw the bridge.
3. Label consonants on the bridge.
4. Choose pattern and break the word.
5. Repeat for any other syllables.
6. Label the syllable.

op        op

gravy

VCV

New Words

gravy                    Brody

slyly                    crazy

Review

lazy                    veto

Break BEFORE you read

gra/vy
Brody
slyly
crazy
lazy
veto

Break WHILE you read

Bro/dy let the students in class play his game.

The rancher slyly snuck up on the bison.

Follow the steps to divide the syllables.
1. Label the first two vowels.
2. Draw the bridge.
3. Label consonants on the bridge.
4. Choose pattern and break the word.
5. Repeat for any other syllables.
6. Label the syllable.

New
Words

gravy                    Brody

slyly                    crazy

Review

lazy                     veto

Break BEFORE you read          Break WHILE you read

gravy
Brody                    Brody let the students
slyly                    in class play his game.
crazy
lazy                     The rancher slyly
veto                     snuck up on the bison.

Follow the steps to divide the syllables.
1. Label the first two vowels.
2. Draw the bridge.
3. Label consonants on the bridge.
4. Choose pattern and break the word.
5. Repeat for any other syllables.
6. Label the syllable.

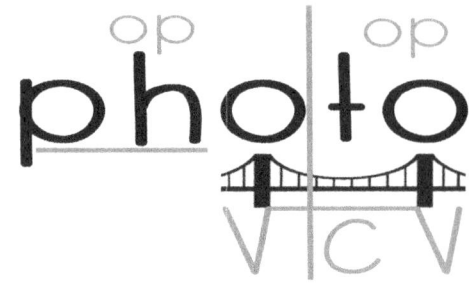

op    op
**photo**
V | C V

New
Words

□ □
photo
[ ]

□ □
shiny
[ ]

□ □
trophy
[ ]

□ □
shaky
[ ]

Review

□ □
Stacy
[ ]

□ □
zero
[ ]

Break BEFORE you read

pho/to
shiny
trophy
shaky
Stacy
zero

Break WHILE you read

Sta/cy took her shiny trophy to the case in the lobby.

Brady was too shaky to take the photo next to the python.

Name: _____

## Follow the steps to divide the syllables.
1. Label the first two vowels.
2. Draw the bridge.
3. Label consonants on the bridge.
4. Choose pattern and break the word.
5. Repeat for any other syllables.
6. Label the syllable.

op        op
**photo**
V | C V

New
Words

**photo**          **shiny**

**trophy**          **shaky**

Review

**Stacy**          **zero**

Break BEFORE you read

pho/to
shiny
trophy
shaky
Stacy
zero

Break WHILE you read

Sta/cy took her shiny trophy to the case in the lobby.

Brady was too shaky to take the photo next to the python.

Follow the steps to divide the syllables.
1. Label the first two vowels.
2. Draw the bridge.
3. Label consonants on the bridge.
4. Choose pattern and break the word.
5. Repeat for any other syllables.
6. Label the syllable.

New Words

photo                shiny

trophy               shaky

Review

Stacy                zero

Break BEFORE you read

photo
shiny
trophy
shaky
Stacy
zero

Break WHILE you read

Stacy took her shiny trophy to the case in the lobby.

Brady was too shaky to take the photo next to the python.

## Follow the steps to divide the syllables.
1. Label the first two vowels.
2. Draw the bridge.
3. Label consonants on the bridge.
4. Choose pattern and break the word.
5. Repeat for any other syllables.
6. Label the syllable.

```
 op  op      cl
c o z i n e s s
  ▥   ▥   ▥
V C V C V
```

New Words

☐ ☐ ☐
## coziness
[          ]

☐ ☐ ☐
## laziness
[          ]

☐ ☐ ☐
## retaken
[          ]

Review

☐   ☐
## promo
[          ]

☐   ☐
## deny
[          ]

☐   ☐
## pogo
[          ]

Break BEFORE you read

co/zi/ness
laziness
retaken
promo
deny
pogo

Break WHILE you read

The stu/dent's laziness did not help him on the chimpanzee essay.

The butterfly test can be retaken next week if you would like to try for a better grade.

Follow the steps to divide the syllables.
1. Label the first two vowels.
2. Draw the bridge.
3. Label consonants on the bridge.
4. Choose pattern and break the word.
5. Repeat for any other syllables.
6. Label the syllable.

op | op | cl
c o z i n e s s
V C V C V

## New Words

coziness

laziness

retaken

## Review

promo

deny

pogo

## Break BEFORE you read

co/zi/ness
laziness
retaken
promo
deny
pogo

## Break WHILE you read

The stu/dent's laziness did not help him on the chimpanzee essay.

The butterfly test can be retaken next week if you would like to try for a better grade.

Follow the steps to divide the syllables.
1. Label the first two vowels.
2. Draw the bridge.
3. Label consonants on the bridge.
4. Choose pattern and break the word.
5. Repeat for any other syllables.
6. Label the syllable.

## New Words

## Review

coziness

promo

laziness

deny

retaken

pogo

Break BEFORE you read

coziness
laziness
retaken
promo
deny
pogo

Break WHILE you read

The student's laziness did not help him on the chimpanzee essay.

The butterfly test can be retaken next week if you would like to try for a better grade.

Follow the steps to divide the syllables.
1. Label the first two vowels.
2. Draw the bridge.
3. Label consonants on the bridge.
4. Choose pattern and break the word.
5. Repeat for any other syllables.
6. Label the syllable.

op | op | cl
reprogram
V|C V|C V

## New Words

reprogram

shadiness

shininess

## Review

shady

shyly

nosy

## Break BEFORE you read

re/pro/gram
shadiness
shininess
shady
shyly
nosy

## Break WHILE you read

We had to re/pro/gram the robot to pick up the stick and move it.

The shadiness of the garden made it hard to take the photo.

Follow the steps to divide the syllables.
1. Label the first two vowels.
2. Draw the bridge.
3. Label consonants on the bridge.
4. Choose pattern and break the word.
5. Repeat for any other syllables.
6. Label the syllable.

op | op | cl

re prog ram

V | C V | C V

## New Words

reprogram

shadiness

shininess

## Review

shady

shyly

nosy

## Break BEFORE you read

re/pro/gram
shadiness
shininess
shady
shyly
nosy

## Break WHILE you read

We had to re/pro/gram the robot to pick up the stick and move it.

The shadiness of the garden made it hard to take the photo.

Follow the steps to divide the syllables.
1. Label the first two vowels.
2. Draw the bridge.
3. Label consonants on the bridge.
4. Choose pattern and break the word.
5. Repeat for any other syllables.
6. Label the syllable.

## New Words

## Review

reprogram

shady

shadiness

shyly

shininess

nosy

## Break BEFORE you read

reprogram
shadiness
shininess
shady
shyly
nosy

## Break WHILE you read

We had to reprogram the robot to pick up the stick and move it.

The shadiness of the garden made it hard to take the photo.

# Activity Set 10

## Syllable Type Focus: Magic E

### Scope and Sequence

| Activity Number | Syllable Pattern | 1st Syllable Type | 2nd Syllable Type | 3rd Syllable Type | Phonics |
|---|---|---|---|---|---|
| 1 | V/CV | Op | ME | X | Single Phonemes |
| 2 | V/CV | Op | ME | X | Blends |
| 3 | V/CV | Op | ME | X | Blends & Digraphs |
| 4 | V/CV | Cl | Op | ME | Single Phonemes |
| 5 | V/CV | Cl | Op | ME | Blends & Digraphs |

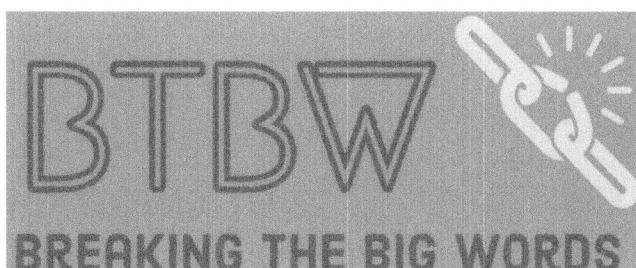

BTBW
BREAKING THE BIG WORDS

Name: _____

Follow the steps to divide the syllables.
1. Label the first two vowels.
2. Draw the bridge.
3. Label consonants on the bridge.
4. Choose pattern and break the word.
5. Repeat for any other syllables.
6. Label the syllable.

op | me
**donate**
V | C V

New
Words

□ □
donate
[ ]

□ □
revise
[ ]

□ □
erase
[ ]

□ □
remote
[ ]

□ □
unite
[ ]

□ □
delete
[ ]

Break BEFORE you read

do/nate
revise
erase
remote
unite
delete

Break WHILE you read

The class will do/nate all sales to unite the lost the kittens.

The pilot had to quickly revise his plans because of the storm.

Follow the steps to divide the syllables.
1. Label the first two vowels.
2. Draw the bridge.
3. Label consonants on the bridge.
4. Choose pattern and break the word.
5. Repeat for any other syllables.
6. Label the syllable.

op   me
# donate
V | C V

donate                    revise

New
Words

erase                     remote

unite                     delete

Break BEFORE you read          Break WHILE you read

do/nate                   The class will do/nate
revise                    all sales to unite the lost
erase                     the kittens.
remote
unite                     The pilot had to quickly
delete                    revise his plans
                          because of the storm.

<u>Follow the steps to divide the syllables.</u>
1. Label the first two vowels.
2. Draw the bridge.
3. Label consonants on the bridge.
4. Choose pattern and break the word.
5. Repeat for any other syllables.
6. Label the syllable.

donate

revise

New
Words

erase

remote

unite

delete

Break BEFORE you read

donate
revise
erase
remote
unite
delete

Break WHILE you read

The class will donate all sales to unite the lost the kittens.

The pilot had to quickly revise his plans because of the storm.

Name: _____

Follow the steps to divide the syllables.
1. Label the first two vowels.
2. Draw the bridge.
3. Label consonants on the bridge.
4. Choose pattern and break the word.
5. Repeat for any other syllables.
6. Label the syllable.

op | me
restate
V | C V

New Words

□ □
prepare
[ ]

□ □
describe
[ ]

□ □
skyline
[ ]

□ □
restate
[ ]

Review

□ □
refuse
[ ]

□ □
reside
[ ]

Break BEFORE you read

pre/pare
describe
skyline
restate
refuse
reside

Break WHILE you read

We should pre/pare for the monthly trip to the west.

Can you describe the skyline when you get there?

Follow the steps to divide the syllables.
1. Label the first two vowels.
2. Draw the bridge.
3. Label consonants on the bridge.
4. Choose pattern and break the word.
5. Repeat for any other syllables.
6. Label the syllable.

op | me
re|state
V | C V

prepare              describe

New
Words

skyline              restate

Review

refuse               reside

Break BEFORE you read        Break WHILE you read

pre/pare            We should pre/pare for
describe            the monthly trip to the
skyline             west.
restate
refuse              Can you describe the
reside              skyline when you get
                    there?

Follow the steps to divide the syllables.
1. Label the first two vowels.
2. Draw the bridge.
3. Label consonants on the bridge.
4. Choose pattern and break the word.
5. Repeat for any other syllables.
6. Label the syllable.

New Words

prepare                    describe

skyline                    restate

Review

refuse                     reside

Break BEFORE you read          Break WHILE you read

prepare                        We should prepare for
describe                       the monthly trip to the
skyline                        west.
restate
refuse                         Can you describe the
reside                         skyline when you get
                               there?

Follow the steps to divide the syllables.
1. Label the first two vowels.
2. Draw the bridge.
3. Label consonants on the bridge.
4. Choose pattern and break the word.
5. Repeat for any other syllables.
6. Label the syllable.

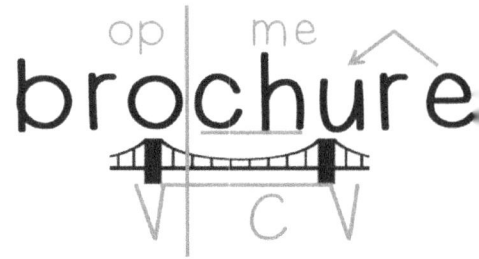

op | me

brochure
V | C | V

New Words

reshave

reshape

Review

beside

brochure

despite

relate

Break BEFORE you read

re/shave
brochure
reshape
despite
beside
relate

Break WHILE you read

The vet had to re/shave the puppy to get out the bubble gum.

We must complete the brochure on China for class.

Follow the steps to divide the syllables.
1. Label the first two vowels.
2. Draw the bridge.
3. Label consonants on the bridge.
4. Choose pattern and break the word.
5. Repeat for any other syllables.
6. Label the syllable.

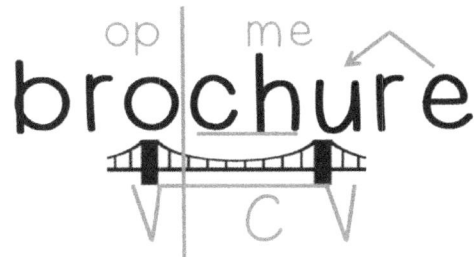

op | me
**bro c hure**
C V

**reshave**

**brochure**

New
Words

**reshape**

**despite**

Review

**beside**

**relate**

Break BEFORE you read

re/shave
brochure
reshape
despite
beside
relate

Break WHILE you read

The vet had to re/shave the puppy to get out the bubble gum.

We must complete the brochure on China for class.

Follow the steps to divide the syllables.
1. Label the first two vowels.
2. Draw the bridge.
3. Label consonants on the bridge.
4. Choose pattern and break the word.
5. Repeat for any other syllables.
6. Label the syllable.

reshave          brochure

New
Words

reshape          despite

Review

beside          relate

Break BEFORE you read

reshave
brochure
reshape
despite
beside
relate

Break WHILE you read

The vet had to reshave the puppy to get out the bubble gum.
We must complete the brochure on China for class.

Name: _____

Follow the steps to divide the syllables.
1. Label the first two vowels.
2. Draw the bridge.
3. Label consonants on the bridge.
4. Choose pattern and break the word.
5. Repeat for any other syllables.
6. Label the syllable.

cl | op | me
incubate
V | C | C | V | C | V

New Words

☐ ☐ ☐

incubate

[box]

☐ ☐ ☐

impolite

[box]

☐ ☐ ☐

calculate

[box]

Review

☐ ☐

refuse

[box]

☐ ☐

supreme

[box]

☐ ☐

produce

[box]

Break BEFORE you read

in/cu/bate
impolite
calculate
refuse
supreme
produce

Break WHILE you read

The ti/ny chicks incubate before they hatch.

He was not impolite, but he had to refuse the snack because there were nuts in it.

53

Name: _____

Follow the steps to divide the syllables.
1. Label the first two vowels.
2. Draw the bridge.
3. Label consonants on the bridge.
4. Choose pattern and break the word.
5. Repeat for any other syllables.
6. Label the syllable.

cl  op  me
incubate
V C C V C V

## New Words

incubate

impolite

calculate

## Review

refuse

supreme

produce

Break BEFORE you read

in/cu/bate
impolite
calculate
refuse
supreme
produce

Break WHILE you read

The ti/ny chicks incubate before they hatch.

He was not impolite, but he had to refuse the snack because there were nuts in it.

Follow the steps to divide the syllables.
1. Label the first two vowels.
2. Draw the bridge.
3. Label consonants on the bridge.
4. Choose pattern and break the word.
5. Repeat for any other syllables.
6. Label the syllable.

Review

New Words

incubate

refuse

impolite

supreme

calculate

produce

Break BEFORE you read

incubate
impolite
calculate
refuse
supreme
produce

Break WHILE you read

The tiny chicks incubate before they hatch.

He was not impolite, but he had to refuse the snack because there were nuts in it.

Follow the steps to divide the syllables.

1. Label the first two vowels.
2. Draw the bridge.
3. Label consonants on the bridge.
4. Choose pattern and break the word.
5. Repeat for any other syllables.
6. Label the syllable.

cl | op | me

compromise

V | C | C | V | C | V

## New Words

☐ ☐ ☐

compromise

☐ ☐ ☐

improvise

☐ ☐ ☐

cellophane

## Review

☐ ☐

reduce

☐ ☐

locate

☐ ☐

device

### Break BEFORE you read

com/pro/mise
improvise
cellophane
reduce
locate
device

### Break WHILE you read

My mom can help us com/pro/mise on which game to play first.

The kids had to improvise to fix the device.

Follow the steps to divide the syllables.
1. Label the first two vowels.
2. Draw the bridge.
3. Label consonants on the bridge.
4. Choose pattern and break the word.
5. Repeat for any other syllables.
6. Label the syllable.

cl   op   me
compromise
V C C V C V

## New Words

compromise

improvise

cellophane

## Review

reduce

locate

device

### Break BEFORE you read

com/pro/mise
improvise
cellophane
reduce
locate
device

### Break WHILE you read

My mom can help us com/pro/mise on which game to play first.

The kids had to improvise to fix the device.

Follow the steps to divide the syllables.
1. Label the first two vowels.
2. Draw the bridge.
3. Label consonants on the bridge.
4. Choose pattern and break the word.
5. Repeat for any other syllables.
6. Label the syllable.

## Review

## New Words

compromise                    reduce

improvise                     locate

cellophane                    device

## Break BEFORE you read        ## Break WHILE you read

compromise                    My mom can help us
improvise                     compromise on which
cellophane                    game to play first.
reduce
locate                        The kids had to
device                        improvise to fix the
                              device.

# Activity Set 11

## Syllable Type Focus: Vowel Pairs

### Scope and Sequence

| Activity Number | Syllable Pattern | 1st Syllable Type | 2nd Syllable Type | 3rd Syllable Type | Phonics |
|---|---|---|---|---|---|
| 1 | V/CV | Op & VP | Op & VP | X | Single Phonemes |
| 2 | V/CV | Op & VP | Cl & VP | X | Blends |
| 3 | V/CV | Op & VP | Cl & VP | X | Blends & Digraphs |
| 4 | V/CV | Cl, Op, & BR | Op & BR | VP | Single Phonemes Blends & Digraphs |
| 5 | V/CV | Op | VP | Cl | |

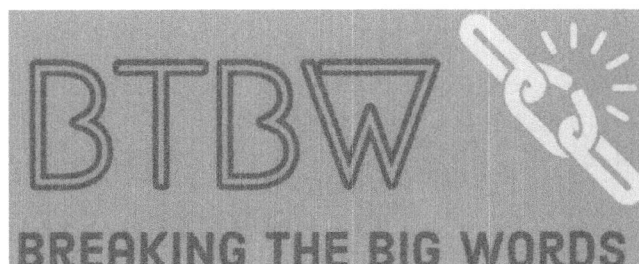

BTBW
BREAKING THE BIG WORDS

VP    VP

## teepee

V | C | V

Follow the steps to divide the syllables.
1. Label the first two vowels.
2. Draw the bridge.
3. Label consonants on the bridge.
4. Choose pattern and break the word.
5. Repeat for any other syllables.
6. Label the syllable.

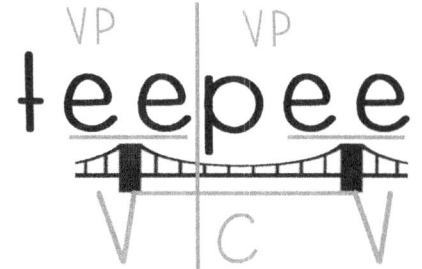

New
Words

teepee

repay

remain

daisy

daily

reveal

## Break BEFORE you read

tee/pee

daisy

repay

daily

remain

reveal

## Break WHILE you read

When we get to Camp Dai/sy can we go inside the teepee?

We need to feed the pony daily so he will remain strong.

## Follow the steps to divide the syllables.
1. Label the first two vowels.
2. Draw the bridge.
3. Label consonants on the bridge.
4. Choose pattern and break the word.
5. Repeat for any other syllables.
6. Label the syllable.

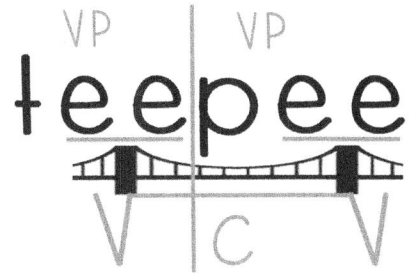

teepee

**teepee**

New
Words

**repay**

**daisy**

**daily**

**remain**

**reveal**

Break BEFORE you read

tee/pee
daisy
repay
daily
remain
reveal

Break WHILE you read

When we get to Camp Daisy can we go inside the teepee?

We need to feed the pony daily so he will remain strong.

Name: _____

Activity 11.1   Version: C

Follow the steps to divide the syllables.
1. Label the first two vowels.
2. Draw the bridge.
3. Label consonants on the bridge.
4. Choose pattern and break the word.
5. Repeat for any other syllables.
6. Label the syllable.

New
Words

teepee                    daisy

repay                     daily

remain                    reveal

Break BEFORE you read        Break WHILE you read

teepee                   When we get to Camp
daisy                    Daisy can we go inside
repay                    the teepee?
daily
remain                   We need to feed the
reveal                   pony daily so he will
                         remain strong.

Follow the steps to divide the syllables.
1. Label the first two vowels.
2. Draw the bridge.
3. Label consonants on the bridge.
4. Choose pattern and break the word.
5. Repeat for any other syllables.
6. Label the syllable.

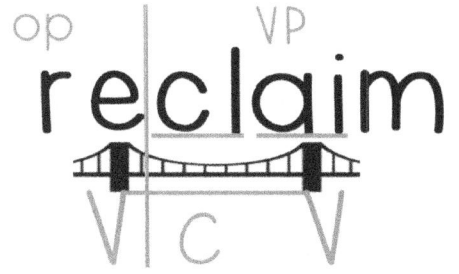

op          VP

re c l aim

V | C   V

□ □
recl aim

New
Words

□ □
proceed

□ □
between

□ □
Friday

Review

□ □
peanut

□ □
repeat

Break BEFORE you read

re/claim
proceed
between
Friday
peanut
repeat

Break WHILE you read

How can we re/claim the time we lost in traffic?

The class can now proceed to line up between the cones.

Follow the steps to divide the syllables.
1. Label the first two vowels.
2. Draw the bridge.
3. Label consonants on the bridge.
4. Choose pattern and break the word.
5. Repeat for any other syllables.
6. Label the syllable.

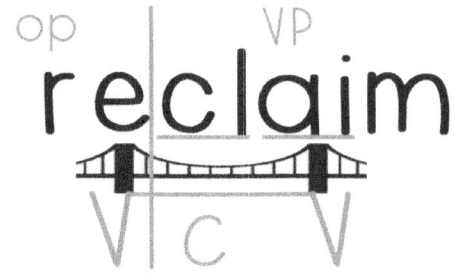

op            VP

re c l ai m

VC   V

reclaim                    proceed

New
Words

between                    Friday

Review

peanut                     repeat

Break BEFORE you read          Break WHILE you read

re/claim                       How can we re/claim
proceed                        the time we lost in
between                        traffic?
Friday
peanut                         The class can now
repeat                         proceed to line up
                               between the cones.

Name: _____

Follow the steps to divide the syllables.
1. Label the first two vowels.
2. Draw the bridge.
3. Label consonants on the bridge.
4. Choose pattern and break the word.
5. Repeat for any other syllables.
6. Label the syllable.

New
Words

reclaim                     proceed

between                     Friday

Review

peanut                      repeat

Break BEFORE you read        Break WHILE you read

reclaim                      How can we reclaim
proceed                      the time we lost in
between                      traffic?
Friday
peanut                       The class can now
repeat                       proceed to line up
                             between the cones.

Follow the steps to divide the syllables.
1. Label the first two vowels.
2. Draw the bridge.
3. Label consonants on the bridge.
4. Choose pattern and break the word.
5. Repeat for any other syllables.
6. Label the syllable.

op    VP
beneath
V|C V

New
Words

□ □
peacock
[    ]

□ □
crayfish
[    ]

□ □
beneath
[    ]

□ □
reteach
[    ]

Review  □ □
teacup
[    ]

□ □
retrain
[    ]

Break BEFORE you read

pea/cock
crayfish
beneath
reteach
teacup
retrain

Break WHILE you read

We will need to re/train the peacock for the contest.

The blue crayfish is beneath the big teacup.

<u>Follow the steps to divide the syllables.</u>
1. Label the first two vowels.
2. Draw the bridge.
3. Label consonants on the bridge.
4. Choose pattern and break the word.
5. Repeat for any other syllables.
6. Label the syllable.

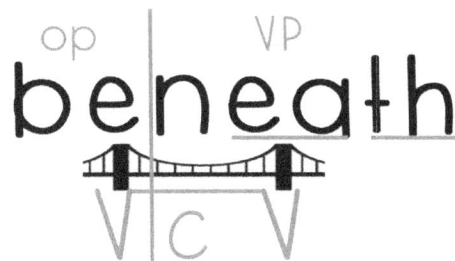

op    VP

be|ne<u>a</u>th

V|C    V

## New Words

<u>pea</u>co<u>c</u>k

<u>cra</u>yfish

ben<u>ea</u>th

ret<u>ea</u>ch

## Review

<u>t</u>e<u>a</u>cup

re<u>t</u>r<u>a</u>in

**Break BEFORE you read**

pea/cock
crayfish
beneath
reteach
teacup
retrain

**Break WHILE you read**

We will need to re/train the peacock for the contest.

The blue crayfish is beneath the big teacup.

Follow the steps to divide the syllables.
1. Label the first two vowels.
2. Draw the bridge.
3. Label consonants on the bridge.
4. Choose pattern and break the word.
5. Repeat for any other syllables.
6. Label the syllable.

New Words

peacock            crayfish

beneath            reteach

Review

teacup             retrain

Break BEFORE you read

peacock
crayfish
beneath
reteach
teacup
retrain

Break WHILE you read

We will need to retrain the peacock for the contest.

The blue crayfish is beneath the big teacup.

Name: _____

## Follow the steps to divide the syllables.
1. Label the first two vowels.
2. Draw the bridge.
3. Label consonants on the bridge.
4. Choose pattern and break the word.
5. Repeat for any other syllables.
6. Label the syllable.

op | BR | VP

over|load

V|C V C C V

## New Words

□ □ □

over<u>load</u>

□ □ □

barbe<u>cue</u>

□ □ □

jambor<u>ee</u>

## Review

□ □

<u>pro</u>cl<u>aim</u>

□ □

red<u>eem</u>

□ □

ret<u>ain</u>

## Break BEFORE you read

o/ver/load
barbecue
jamboree
proclaim
redeem
retain

## Break WHILE you read

Did you o/ver/load the barbecue with meat?

How did you overhear the theme of this year's jamboree?

Follow the steps to divide the syllables.
1. Label the first two vowels.
2. Draw the bridge.
3. Label consonants on the bridge.
4. Choose pattern and break the word.
5. Repeat for any other syllables.
6. Label the syllable.

op | BR | VP
**over|load**
V|C V|C C V

## New Words

overl<u>oa</u>d

barbec<u>ue</u>

jambor<u>ee</u>

## Review

<u>pro</u><u>c</u>l<u>ai</u>m

red<u>ee</u>m

ret<u>ai</u>n

### Break BEFORE you read

o/ver/load
barbecue
jamboree
proclaim
redeem
retain

### Break WHILE you read

Did you o/ver/load the barbecue with meat?

How did you overhear the theme of this year's jamboree?

Follow the steps to divide the syllables.
1. Label the first two vowels.
2. Draw the bridge.
3. Label consonants on the bridge.
4. Choose pattern and break the word.
5. Repeat for any other syllables.
6. Label the syllable.

New Words                    Review

overload        proclaim

barbecue        redeem

jamboree        retain

Break BEFORE you read        Break WHILE you read

overload                     Did you overload the
barbecue                     barbecue with meat?
jamboree
proclaim                     How did you overhear
redeem                       the theme of this year's
retain                       jamboree?

Name: _____

## Follow the steps to divide the syllables.
1. Label the first two vowels.
2. Draw the bridge.
3. Label consonants on the bridge.
4. Choose pattern and break the word.
5. Repeat for any other syllables.
6. Label the syllable.

op | VP | cl

re pay ment

VC V C V

## New Words

□ □ □
repayment
[          ]

□ □ □
pretreatment
[          ]

□ □ □
detainment
[          ]

## Review

□ □
bequeath
[          ]

□ □
protein
[          ]

□ □
detail
[          ]

## Break BEFORE you read

re/pay/ment
pretreatment
detainment
bequeath
protein
detail

## Break WHILE you read

I got you this snack as re/pay/ment for your help with the octopus photograph.

With pretreatment, the stain came out of his shirt.

Follow the steps to divide the syllables.
1. Label the first two vowels.
2. Draw the bridge.
3. Label consonants on the bridge.
4. Choose pattern and break the word.
5. Repeat for any other syllables.
6. Label the syllable.

op | VP | cl

re**p**ay**men**t

V|C V|C V

## New Words

repayment

pretreatment

detainment

## Review

bequeath

protein

detail

## Break BEFORE you read

re/pay/ment
pretreatment
detainment
bequeath
protein
detail

## Break WHILE you read

I got you this snack as re/pay/ment for your help with the octopus photograph.

With pretreatment, the stain came out of his shirt.

Follow the steps to divide the syllables.
1. Label the first two vowels.
2. Draw the bridge.
3. Label consonants on the bridge.
4. Choose pattern and break the word.
5. Repeat for any other syllables.
6. Label the syllable.

New Words

Review

repayment          bequeath

pretreatment          protein

detainment          detail

Break BEFORE you read

repayment
pretreatment
detainment
bequeath
protein
detail

Break WHILE you read

I got you this snack as repayment for your help with the octopus photograph.

With pretreatment, the stain came out of his shirt.

# Activity Set
# 12

# Syllable Type Focus: Bossy R /er/

## Scope and Sequence

| Activity Number | Syllable Pattern | 1st Syllable Type | 2nd Syllable Type | 3rd Syllable Type | Phonics |
|---|---|---|---|---|---|
| 1 | V/CV | Op & VP | BR | X | Single Phonemes |
| 2 | V/CV | Op & VP | BR | X | Blends |
| 3 | V/CV | Op & VP | BR | X | Blends & Digraphs |
| 4 | V/CV | Cl & Op | Op & VP | BR | Single Phonemes Blends & Digraphs |
| 5 | V/CV | Op & BR | Cl, Op, & BR | Cl & BR | |

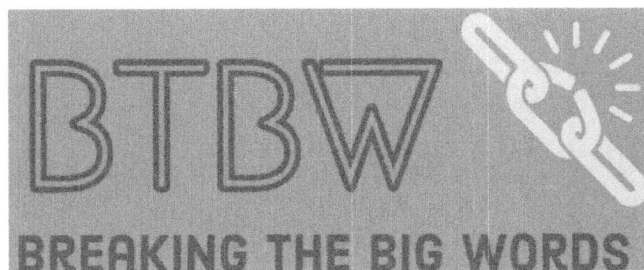

BTBW
BREAKING THE BIG WORDS

Name: _____

Follow the steps to divide the syllables.
1. Label the first two vowels.
2. Draw the bridge.
3. Label consonants on the bridge.
4. Choose pattern and break the word.
5. Repeat for any other syllables.
6. Label the syllable.

op    BR
paper
V C V

New Words

□ □
paper
[    ]

□ □
solar
[    ]

□ □
motor
[    ]

□ □
ruler
[    ]

□ □
waiter
[    ]

□ □
laser
[    ]

Break BEFORE you read

pa/per
ruler
solar
waiter
motor
laser

Break WHILE you read

I need pa/per and a ruler to start my solar system for class.

The waiter at the hotel gave us a motor for the old bike.

Follow the steps to divide the syllables.
1. Label the first two vowels.
2. Draw the bridge.
3. Label consonants on the bridge.
4. Choose pattern and break the word.
5. Repeat for any other syllables.
6. Label the syllable.

op    BR
pa|per
V|C V

paper                    ruler

New
Words

solar                    waiter

motor                    laser

Break BEFORE you read        Break WHILE you read

pa/per                       I need pa/per and a
ruler                        ruler to start my solar
solar                        system for class.
waiter
motor                        The waiter at the hotel
laser                        gave us a motor for the
                             old bike.

Name: _____

Activity 12.1   Version: C

Follow the steps to divide the syllables.
1. Label the first two vowels.
2. Draw the bridge.
3. Label consonants on the bridge.
4. Choose pattern and break the word.
5. Repeat for any other syllables.
6. Label the syllable.

New
Words

paper

ruler

solar

waiter

motor

laser

Break BEFORE you read

paper
ruler
solar
waiter
motor
laser

Break WHILE you read

I need paper and a ruler to start my solar system for class.

The waiter at the hotel gave us a motor for the old bike.

Name: _____

## Follow the steps to divide the syllables.
1. Label the first two vowels.
2. Draw the bridge.
3. Label consonants on the bridge.
4. Choose pattern and break the word.
5. Repeat for any other syllables.
6. Label the syllable.

op   BR
**spi|der**
V C V

New
Words

□ □
spider
[ ]

□ □
record
[ ]

□ □
trainer
[ ]

□ □
flavor
[ ]

Review

□ □
later
[ ]

□ □
tiger
[ ]

Break BEFORE you read

spi/der
record
trainer
flavor
later
tiger

Break WHILE you read

When we see the spi/der we need to record the number of spots and length.

Will the trainer return the tiger to us by Friday?

79

Activity 12.2    Version: B

# Follow the steps to divide the syllables.

1. Label the first two vowels.
2. Draw the bridge.
3. Label consonants on the bridge.
4. Choose pattern and break the word.
5. Repeat for any other syllables.
6. Label the syllable.

op | BR
spi|der

V | C V

spider                record

New
Words

trainer               flavor

Review

later                 tiger

Break BEFORE you read

spi/der
record
trainer
flavor
later
tiger

Break WHILE you read

When we see the spi/der we need to record the number of spots and length.

Will the trainer return the tiger to us by Friday?

<u>Follow the steps to divide the syllables.</u>
1. Label the first two vowels.
2. Draw the bridge.
3. Label consonants on the bridge.
4. Choose pattern and break the word.
5. Repeat for any other syllables.
6. Label the syllable.

New
Words

spider

record

trainer

flavor

Review

later

tiger

Break BEFORE you read

spider
record
trainer
flavor
later
tiger

Break WHILE you read

When we see the spider we need to record the number of spots and length.

Will the trainer return the tiger to us by Friday?

Follow the steps to divide the syllables.
1. Label the first two vowels.
2. Draw the bridge.
3. Label consonants on the bridge.
4. Choose pattern and break the word.
5. Repeat for any other syllables.
6. Label the syllable.

VP    BR
teacher
V    C    V

**New Words**

teacher

bleachers

preacher

neither

**Review**

razor

clover

Break BEFORE you read

tea/cher
bleachers
preacher
neither
razor
clover

Break WHILE you read

Ask the tea/cher if we can return the starfish to the seashore this morning?
There was a tiny rodent under the bleachers yesterday.

Follow the steps to divide the syllables.
1. Label the first two vowels.
2. Draw the bridge.
3. Label consonants on the bridge.
4. Choose pattern and break the word.
5. Repeat for any other syllables.
6. Label the syllable.

VP | BR
teacher
V | C V

**New Words**

teacher                    bleachers

preacher                   neither

**Review**

razor                      clover

Break BEFORE you read          Break WHILE you read

tea/cher                       Ask the tea/cher if we
bleachers                      can return the starfish
preacher                       to the seashore this
neither                        morning?
razor                          There was a tiny
clover                         rodent under the
                               bleachers yesterday.

Follow the steps to divide the syllables.
1. Label the first two vowels.
2. Draw the bridge.
3. Label consonants on the bridge.
4. Choose pattern and break the word.
5. Repeat for any other syllables.
6. Label the syllable.

## teacher                    bleachers

New
Words

## preacher                   neither

Review

## razor                      clover

Break BEFORE you read          Break WHILE you read

teacher                        Ask the teacher if we
bleachers                      can return the starfish
preacher                       to the seashore this
neither                        morning?
razor                          There was a tiny
clover                         rodent under the
                               bleachers yesterday.

Follow the steps to divide the syllables.
1. Label the first two vowels.
2. Draw the bridge.
3. Label consonants on the bridge.
4. Choose pattern and break the word.
5. Repeat for any other syllables.
6. Label the syllable.

cl | op | BR
computer
VC|C|VC|C|V

## New Words

☐ ☐ ☐
rem**ai**nder

☐ ☐ ☐
computer

☐ ☐ ☐
eraser

## Review

☐ ☐
st**a**pler

☐ ☐
cr**a**ter

☐ ☐
sup**e**rb

### Break BEFORE you read
re/main/der
computer
eraser
stapler
crater
superb

### Break WHILE you read
I spent the re/main/der of the day on the computer.

Did you see my gigantic eraser shaped like a torpedo?

Name: _____

Follow the steps to divide the syllables.
1. Label the first two vowels.
2. Draw the bridge.
3. Label consonants on the bridge.
4. Choose pattern and break the word.
5. Repeat for any other syllables.
6. Label the syllable.

cl  op  BR
computer
VCCVCV

## New Words

rem**a**inder

computer

eraser

## Review

st**a**p**l**er

c**r**ater

supe**rb**

## Break BEFORE you read

re/main/der
computer
eraser
stapler
crater
superb

## Break WHILE you read

I spent the re/main/der of the day on the computer.

Did you see my gigantic eraser shaped like a torpedo?

Name: _____

Follow the steps to divide the syllables.

1. Label the first two vowels.
2. Draw the bridge.
3. Label consonants on the bridge.
4. Choose pattern and break the word.
5. Repeat for any other syllables.
6. Label the syllable.

## New Words

## Review

remainder

stapler

computer

crater

eraser

superb

Break BEFORE you read

remainder
computer
eraser
stapler
crater
superb

Break WHILE you read

I spent the remainder of the day on the computer.

Did you see my gigantic eraser shaped like a torpedo?

Name: _____

## Follow the steps to divide the syllables.

1. Label the first two vowels.
2. Draw the bridge.
3. Label consonants on the bridge.
4. Choose pattern and break the word.
5. Repeat for any other syllables.
6. Label the syllable.

BR | op | cl

turbulent

VCVCV

Review

## New Words

turbulent

propeller

department

baker

liner

savor

Break BEFORE you read

tur/bu/lent
propeller
department
baker
liner
savor

Break WHILE you read

It was a tur/bu/lent ride due to the frozen propeller.

We can get a frame for the photograph at the department store.

Name: _____

Follow the steps to divide the syllables.
1. Label the first two vowels.
2. Draw the bridge.
3. Label consonants on the bridge.
4. Choose pattern and break the word.
5. Repeat for any other syllables.
6. Label the syllable.

BR | op | cl
# turbulent
V|C|C V|C|C V

## New Words

turbule<u>nt</u>

<u>pr</u>opeller

depa<u>r</u><u>t</u>me<u>n</u>t

## Review

baker

liner

savor

## Break BEFORE you read

tur/bu/lent
propeller
department
baker
liner
savor

## Break WHILE you read

It was a tur/bu/lent ride due to the frozen propeller.

We can get a frame for the photograph at the department store.

Follow the steps to divide the syllables.
1. Label the first two vowels.
2. Draw the bridge.
3. Label consonants on the bridge.
4. Choose pattern and break the word.
5. Repeat for any other syllables.
6. Label the syllable.

New Words

Review

turbulent

baker

propeller

liner

department

savor

Break BEFORE you read

turbulent
propeller
department
baker
liner
savor

Break WHILE you read

It was a turbulent ride due to the frozen propeller.

We can get a frame for the photograph at the department store.

# Activity Set 13

# Syllable Type Focus: Consonant-le

## Scope and Sequence

| Activity Number | Syllable Pattern | 1st Syllable Type | 2nd Syllable Type | 3rd Syllable Type | Phonics |
|---|---|---|---|---|---|
| 1 | V/CV | Op & VP | C-le | X | Single Phonemes |
| 2 | V/CV | Op & VP | C-le | X | Blends |
| 3 | V/CV | Op & VP | Cl & Op | X | Blends |
| 4 | V/CV | Op & VP | Cl & Op | C-le | Single Phonemes |
| 5 | V/CV | Cl & Op | Cl & Op | C-le | Blends & Digraphs |

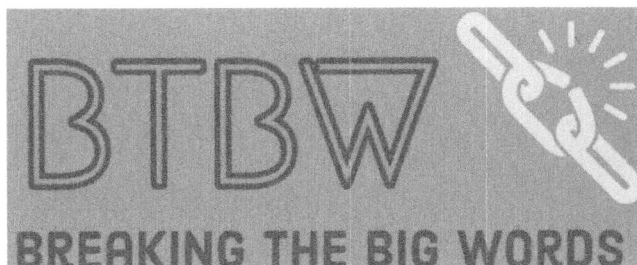

BTBW
BREAKING THE BIG WORDS

Follow the steps to divide the syllables.
1. Label the first two vowels.
2. Draw the bridge.
3. Label consonants on the bridge.
4. Choose pattern and break the word.
5. Repeat for any other syllables.
6. Label the syllable.

VP | C-le
**beagle**
V | C V

New Words

beagle

people

eagle

able

maple

needle

Break BEFORE you read

bea/gle
able
people
maple
eagle
needle

Break WHILE you read

Ja/cob's beagle was able to help the people.

The students can wait under the maple to see the eagle?

Follow the steps to divide the syllables.
1. Label the first two vowels.
2. Draw the bridge.
3. Label consonants on the bridge.
4. Choose pattern and break the word.
5. Repeat for any other syllables.
6. Label the syllable.

VP    C-le

beagle

V    C V

beagle                          able

New
Words

people                          maple

eagle                           needle

Break BEFORE you read        Break WHILE you read

bea/gle                      Jacob's beagle was
able                         able to help the people.
people
maple                        The students can wait
eagle                        under the maple to see
needle                       the eagle?

Follow the steps to divide the syllables.
1. Label the first two vowels.
2. Draw the bridge.
3. Label consonants on the bridge.
4. Choose pattern and break the word.
5. Repeat for any other syllables.
6. Label the syllable.

New
Words

# beagle            able

# people            maple

# eagle             needle

Break BEFORE you read        Break WHILE you read

beagle

able                    Jacob's beagle was
                        able to help the people.
people

maple                   The students can wait
                        under the maple to see
eagle                   the eagle?

needle

Follow the steps to divide the syllables.
1. Label the first two vowels.
2. Draw the bridge.
3. Label consonants on the bridge.
4. Choose pattern and break the word.
5. Repeat for any other syllables.
6. Label the syllable.

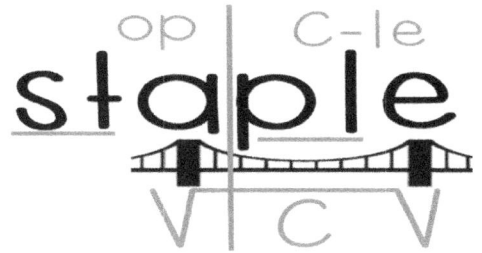

op | C-le
**staple**
V | C V

New Words

□ □
**bridle**
[ ]

□ □
**stable**
[ ]

□ □
**fable**
[ ]

□ □
**staple**
[ ]

Review

□ □
**beetle**
[ ]

□ □
**bugle**
[ ]

Break BEFORE you read

bri/dle
stable
fable
staple
beetle
bugle

Break WHILE you read

Bra/dy went to get the bridle while the students remained in the stable.

Were you able to get the staple out of the paper?

Name: _____

Follow the steps to divide the syllables.
1. Label the first two vowels.
2. Draw the bridge.
3. Label consonants on the bridge.
4. Choose pattern and break the word.
5. Repeat for any other syllables.
6. Label the syllable.

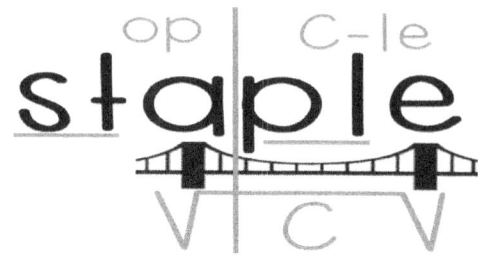

op   C-le
st**a**p**le**
V   C   V

## New Words

bri**dl**e

st**ab**le

f**ab**le

st**ap**le

## Review

b**ee**tle

bu**gl**e

Break BEFORE you read

bri/dle
stable
fable
staple
beetle
bugle

Break WHILE you read

Bra/dy went to get the bridle while the students remained in the stable.

Were you able to get the staple out of the paper?

Follow the steps to divide the syllables.
1. Label the first two vowels.
2. Draw the bridge.
3. Label consonants on the bridge.
4. Choose pattern and break the word.
5. Repeat for any other syllables.
6. Label the syllable.

New
Words

bridle                     stable

fable                      staple

Review

beetle                     bugle

Break BEFORE you read      Break WHILE you read

bridle                     Brady went to get the
stable                     bridle while the
fable                      students remained in
staple                     the stable.
beetle
bugle                      Were you able to get
                           the staple out of the
                           paper?

Name: _____

## Follow the steps to divide the syllables.
1. Label the first two vowels.
2. Draw the bridge.
3. Label consonants on the bridge.
4. Choose pattern and break the word.
5. Repeat for any other syllables.
6. Label the syllable.

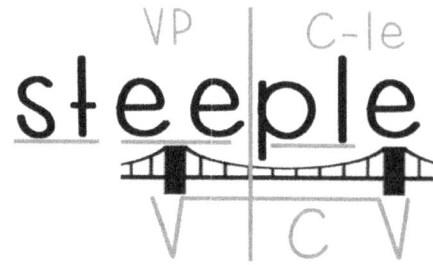

VP | C-le

steeple

V | C V

New Words

steeple

stifle

trifle

scruple

Review

gable

cable

Break BEFORE you read

stee/ple
stifle
trifle
scruple
gable
cable

Break WHILE you read

How long will it take to re/store the church's steeple?

She tried to stifle a grin as the beetle surprised her brother.

98

Follow the steps to divide the syllables.
1. Label the first two vowels.
2. Draw the bridge.
3. Label consonants on the bridge.
4. Choose pattern and break the word.
5. Repeat for any other syllables.
6. Label the syllable.

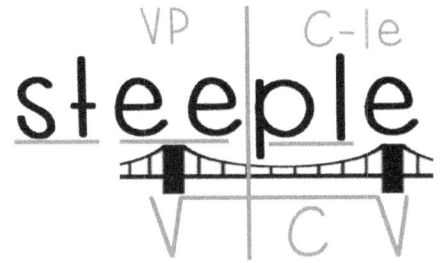

VP | C-le

## steeple

VCV

**New Words**

## steeple

## stifle

## trifle

## scruple

**Review**

## gable

## cable

Break BEFORE you read

stee/ple
stifle
trifle
scruple
gable
cable

Break WHILE you read

How long will it take to re/store the church's steeple?

She tried to stifle a grin as the beetle surprised her brother.

Name: _____   Activity 13.3    Version: C

Follow the steps to divide the syllables.
1. Label the first two vowels.
2. Draw the bridge.
3. Label consonants on the bridge.
4. Choose pattern and break the word.
5. Repeat for any other syllables.
6. Label the syllable.

**steeple**        **stifle**

New
Words

**trifle**        **scruple**

Review

**gable**        **cable**

Break BEFORE you read          Break WHILE you read

steeple
stifle
trifle
scruple
gable
cable

How long will it take to restore the church's steeple?

She tried to stifle a grin as the beetle surprised her brother.

Name: _____

Follow the steps to divide the syllables.
1. Label the first two vowels.
2. Draw the bridge.
3. Label consonants on the bridge.
4. Choose pattern and break the word.
5. Repeat for any other syllables.
6. Label the syllable.

op | op | C-le
**recycle**
V|C V|C V

## New Words

teakettle

resemble

recycle

## Review

cycle

idle

table

**Break BEFORE you read**
tea/ket/tle
resemble
recycle
cycle
idle
table

**Break WHILE you read**
Did you see the tea/ket/tle that resembles an eagle?

We can recycle all of that paper into garden mulch.

101

Follow the steps to divide the syllables.
1. Label the first two vowels.
2. Draw the bridge.
3. Label consonants on the bridge.
4. Choose pattern and break the word.
5. Repeat for any other syllables.
6. Label the syllable.

op | op | C-le
**recycle**
V|C V|C V

## New Words

t**ea**ke**tt**le

resem**ble**

recy**cle**

## Review

cy**cl**e

i**dl**e

ta**bl**e

Break BEFORE you read

tea/ket/tle
resemble
recycle
cycle
idle
table

Break WHILE you read

Did you see the tea/ket/tle that resembles an eagle?

We can recycle all of that paper into garden mulch.

Follow the steps to divide the syllables.
1. Label the first two vowels.
2. Draw the bridge.
3. Label consonants on the bridge.
4. Choose pattern and break the word.
5. Repeat for any other syllables.
6. Label the syllable.

## New Words

teakettle

resemble

recycle

## Review

cycle

idle

table

## Break BEFORE you read

teakettle
resemble
recycle
cycle
idle
table

## Break WHILE you read

Did you see the teakettle that resembles an eagle?

We can recycle all of that paper into garden mulch.

Name: _____

Follow the steps to divide the syllables.
1. Label the first two vowels.
2. Draw the bridge.
3. Label consonants on the bridge.
4. Choose pattern and break the word.
5. Repeat for any other syllables.
6. Label the syllable.

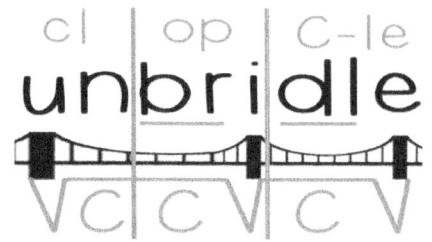

cl | op | C-le
unbridle
VC | C V | C V

## New Words

reshuffle

unbridle

resample

## Review

ladle

title

sidle

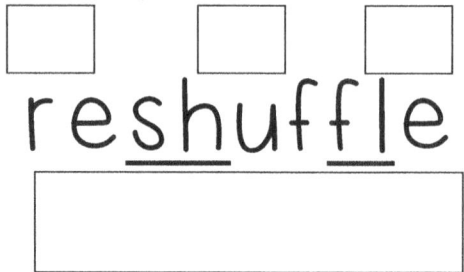

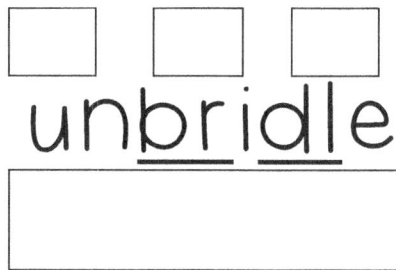

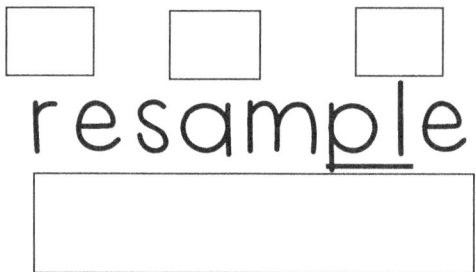

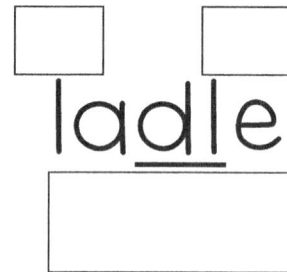

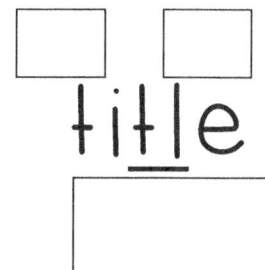

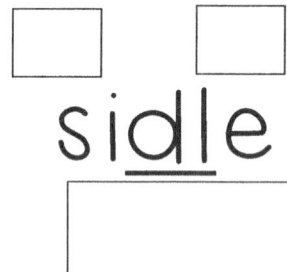

## Break BEFORE you read

re/shuf/fle
unbridle
resample
ladle
title
sidle

## Break WHILE you read

We will need to re/shuf/fle the cards before we play again.

After we unbridle the pony in the stable we can go to the lake.

Follow the steps to divide the syllables.
1. Label the first two vowels.
2. Draw the bridge.
3. Label consonants on the bridge.
4. Choose pattern and break the word.
5. Repeat for any other syllables.
6. Label the syllable.

cl | op | C-le
## unbridle
V C | C V | C V

## New Words

reshuffle

unbridle

resample

## Review

ladle

title

sidle

## Break BEFORE you read

re/shuf/fle
unbridle
resample
ladle
title
sidle

## Break WHILE you read

We will need to re/shuf/fle the cards before we play again.

After we unbridle the pony in the stable we can go to the lake.

<u>Follow the steps to divide the syllables.</u>
1. Label the first two vowels.
2. Draw the bridge.
3. Label consonants on the bridge.
4. Choose pattern and break the word.
5. Repeat for any other syllables.
6. Label the syllable.

## New Words

## Review

reshuffle

ladle

unbridle

title

resample

sidle

## Break BEFORE you read

reshuffle
unbridle
resample
ladle
title
sidle

## Break WHILE you read

We will need to reshuffle the cards before we play again.

After we unbridle the pony in the stable we can go to the lake.

# Activity Set
# 8

## Syllabication Anchor Word Posters

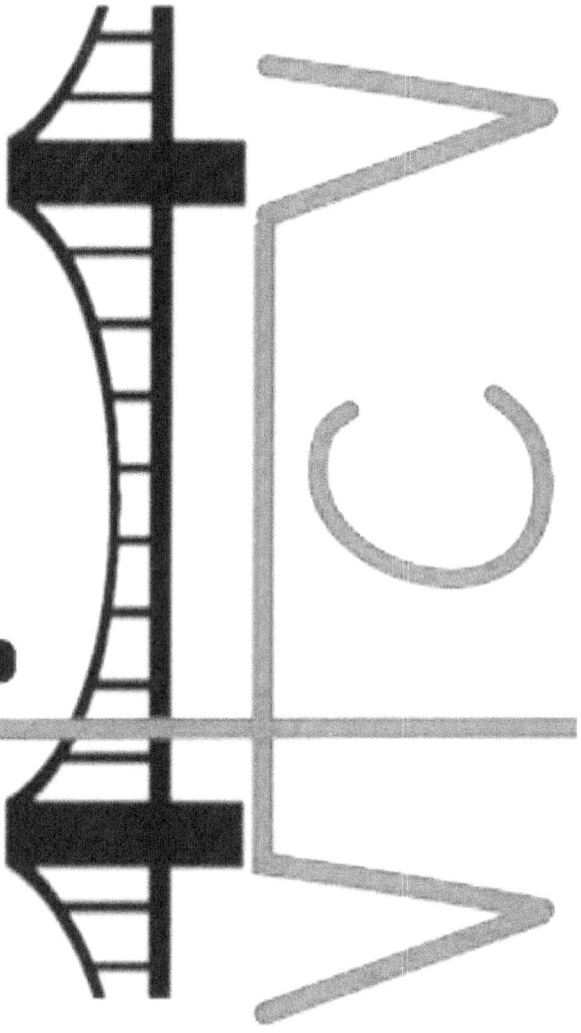

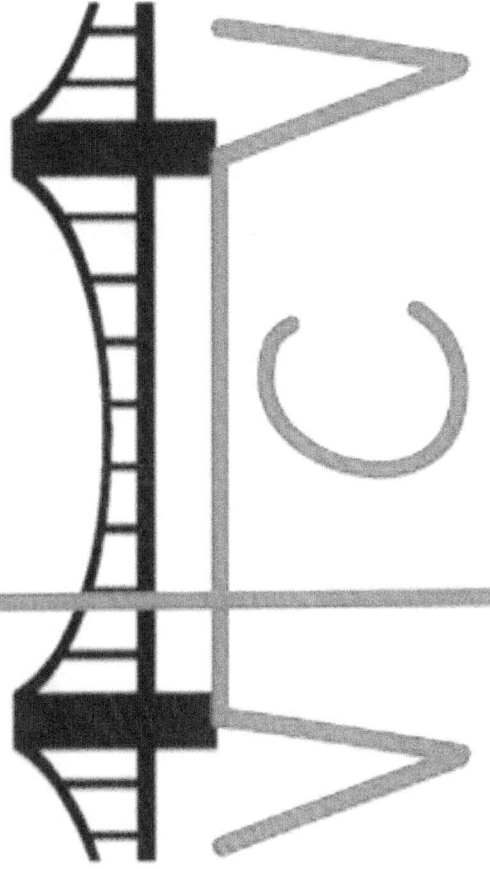

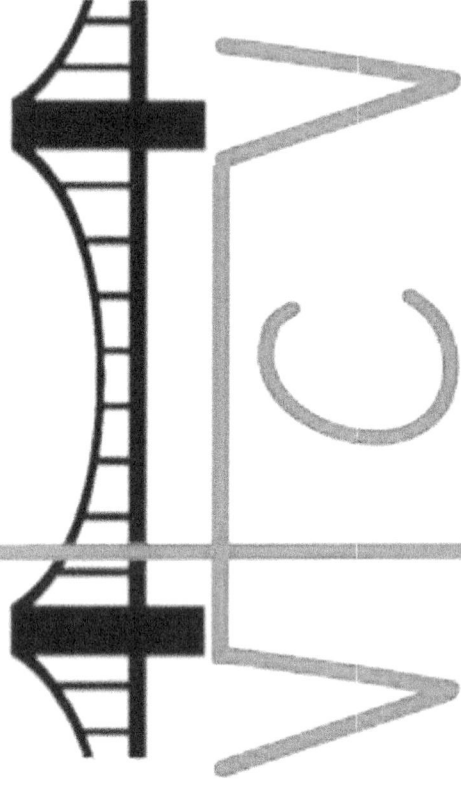

studentsVIC

photograph

ph o t o g r a ph

VC CVC CVC

# Activity Set
# 9

# Syllabication Anchor Word Posters

photo

coziness

ci op op op

VC CVC CVC VC

reprogram

# Activity Set

# 10

## Syllabication Anchor Word Posters

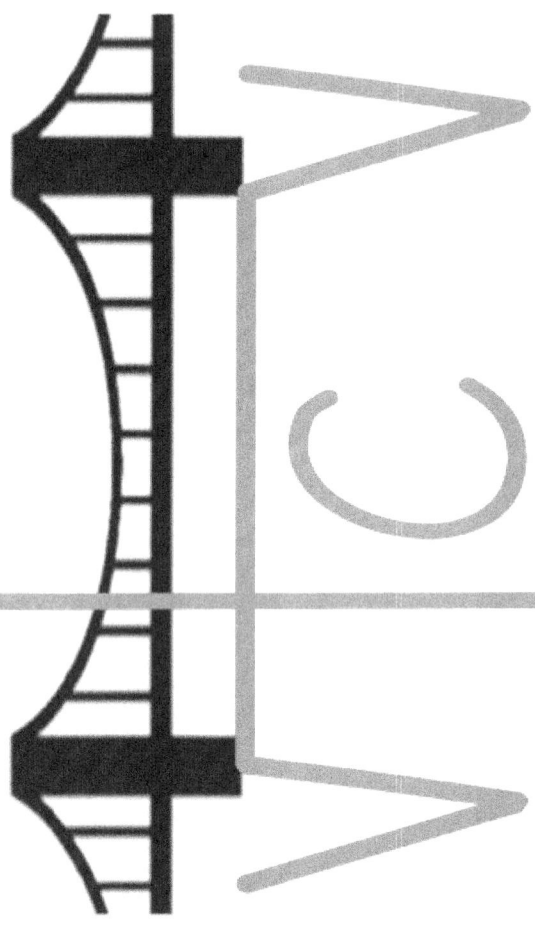

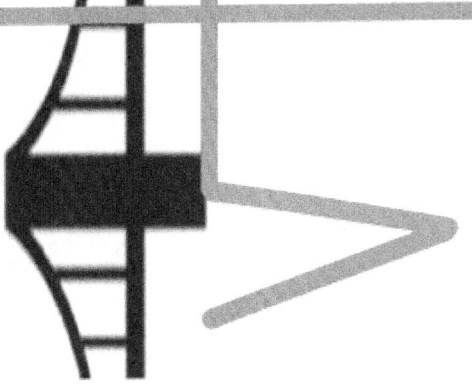

real estate

brochure

.incubate

climate

develop

VCC VCC CVC

# Activity Set
# 11

Syllabication
Anchor Word
Posters

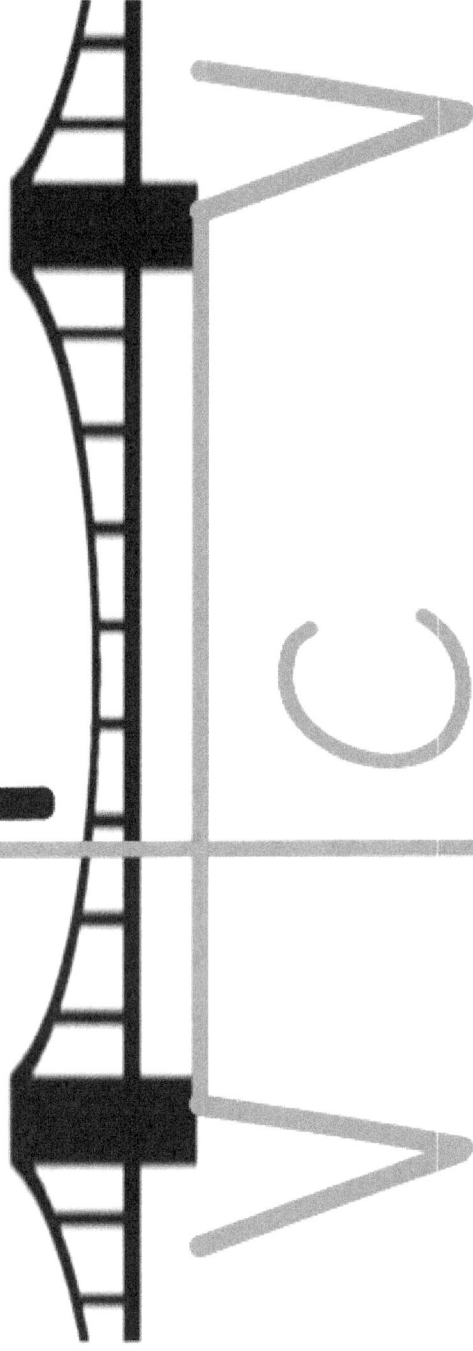

teepee

VP

VP

VP

VC

beneath

health

VP
op
Vic
c

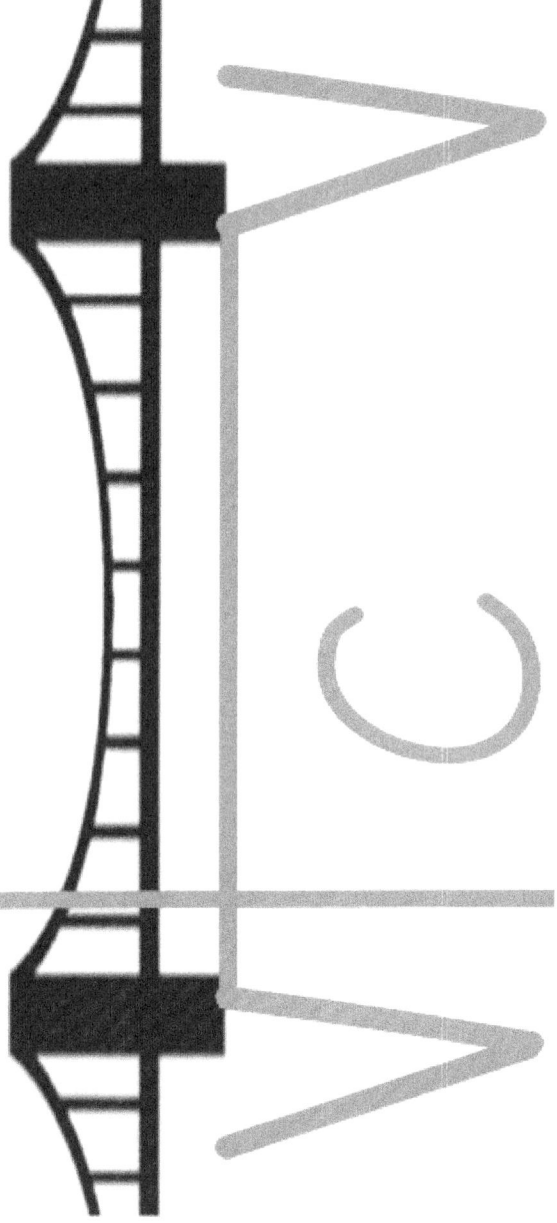

reclaim

VIC

VP

op

op BR VP

over load

cvc cvcc

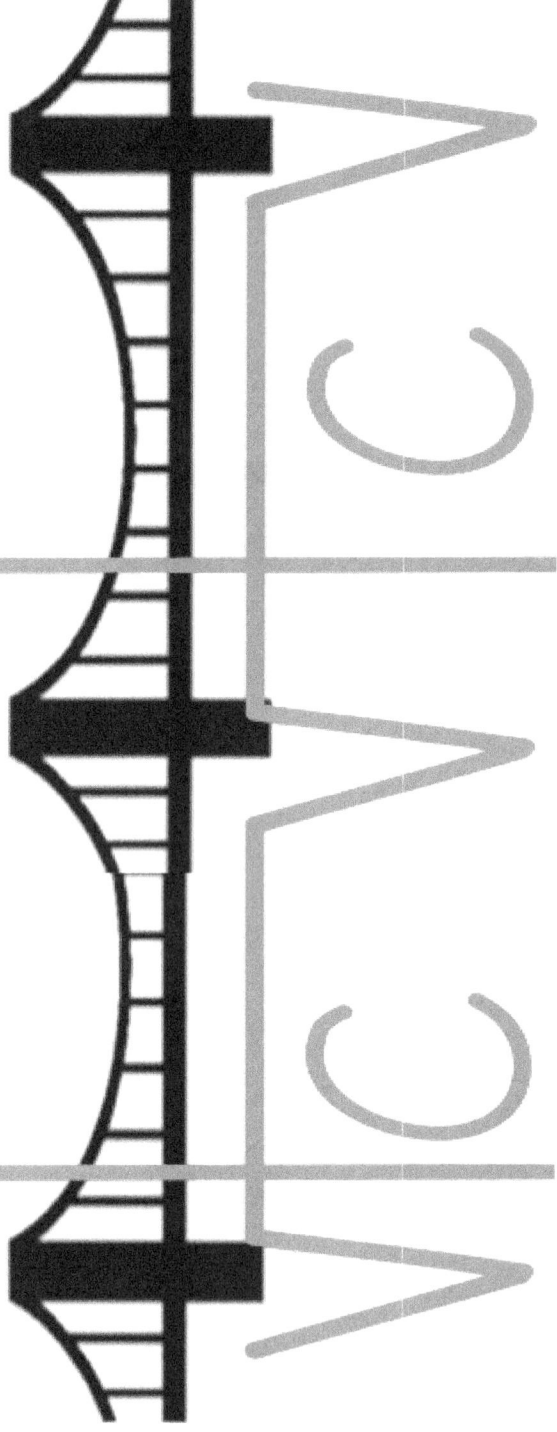

# repayment

op vp cl cl vp op

# Activity Set

# 12

# Syllabication Anchor Word Posters

paper

BR op VIC

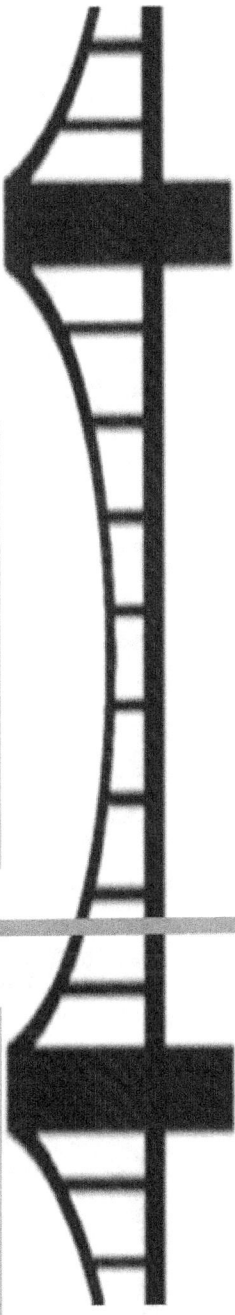

teacher

VP BR
VP C

cl

op BR

computer

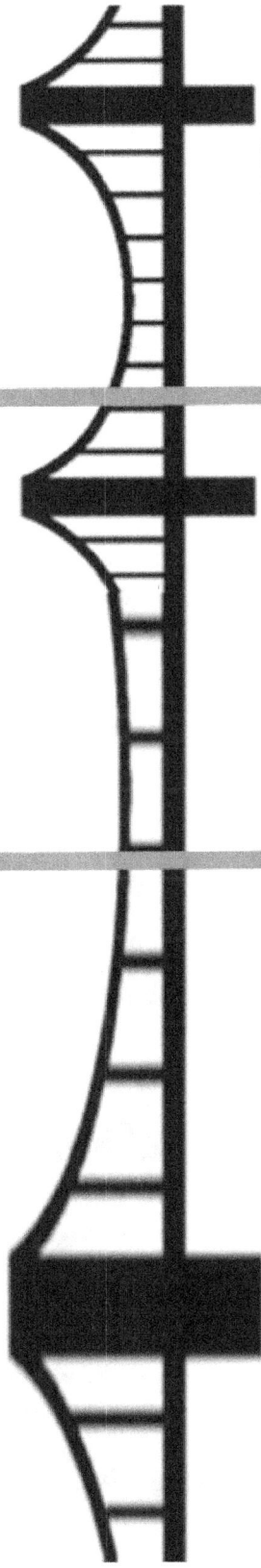

cvlc cvlc

turbulent

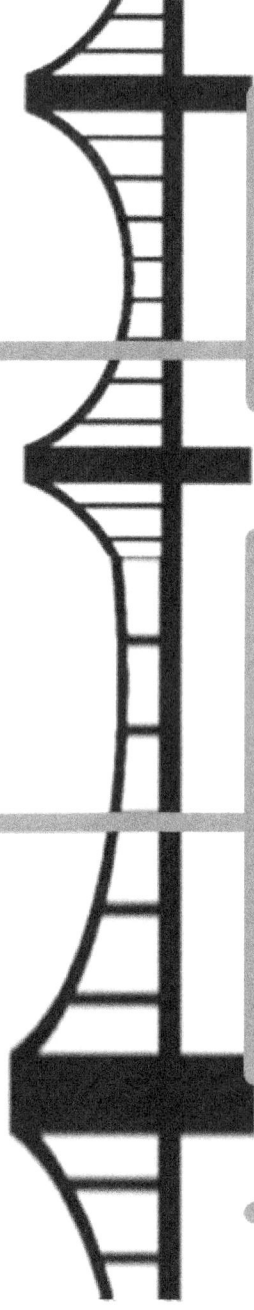

VCVCVC  CVCCVC

# Activity Set

# 13

# Syllabication Anchor Word Posters

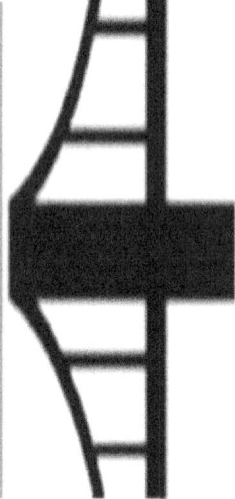

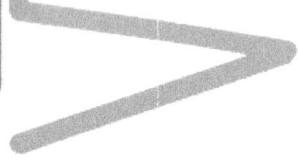

eagle
beagle

VP c-le
VP c

steeple

VP

C-le

C

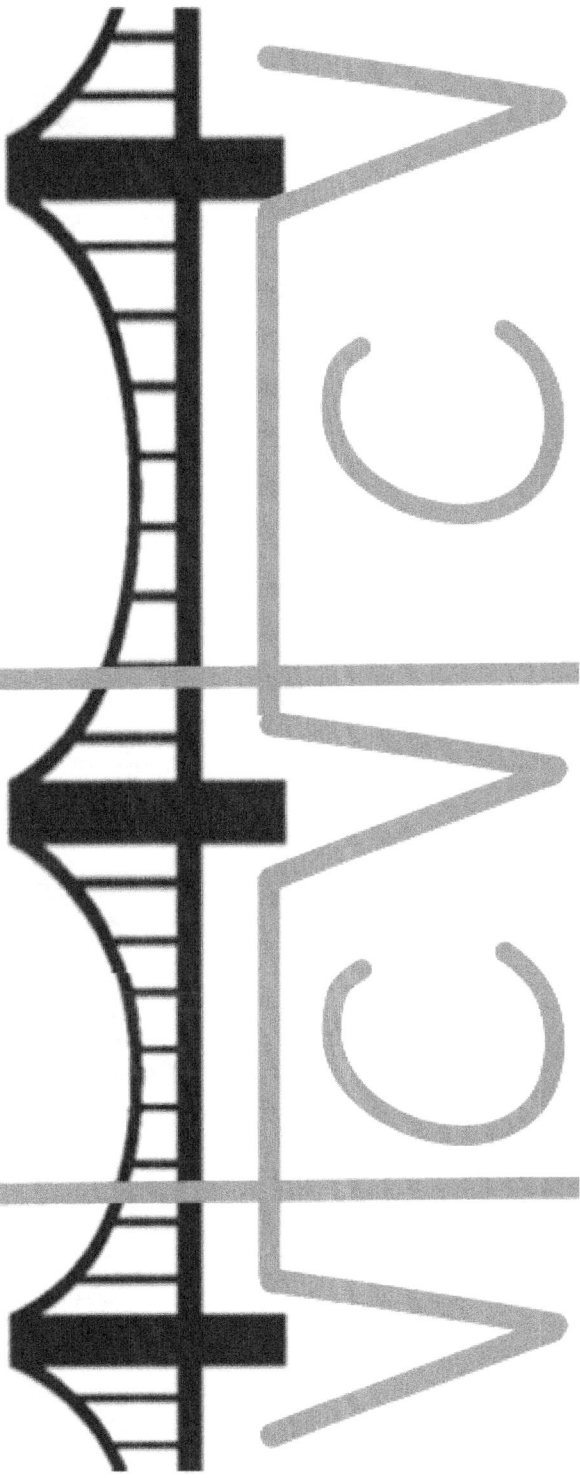

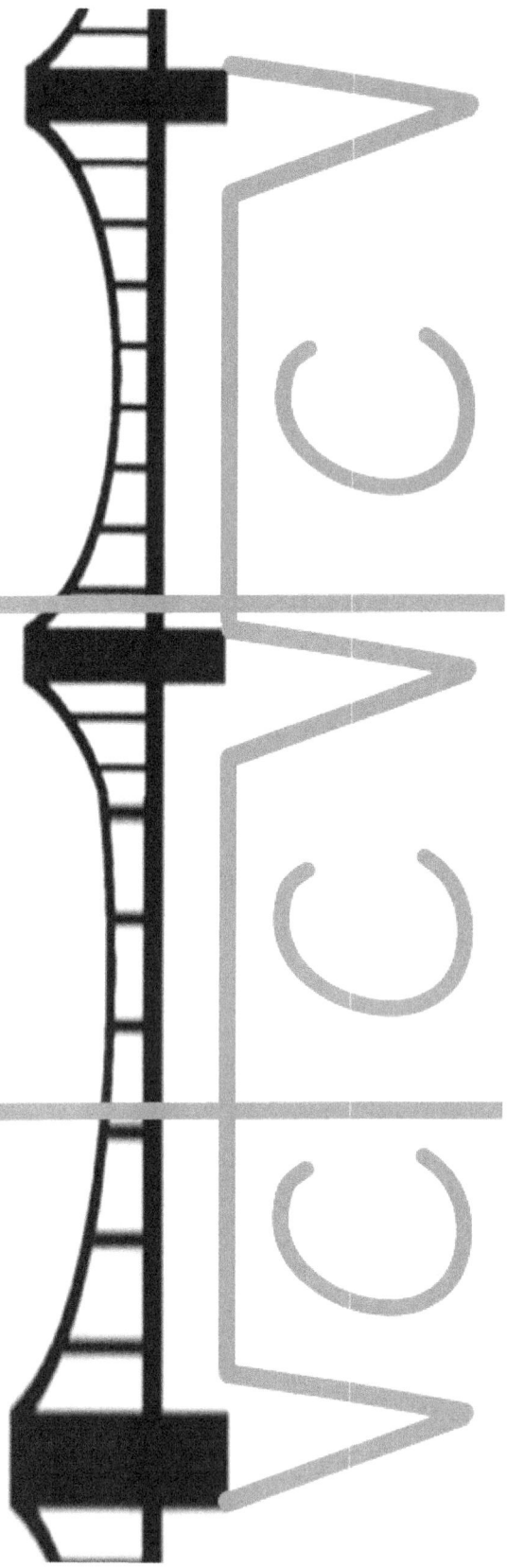

c-le   c-le

op   op

cl   cl

unbridle

CVC CVC CVCVC

# Vowel Types

| Long | Short | Tricksters |
|---|---|---|
| Name of vowel | Sound of vowel | Different |
| wait   line   so | hat   up   top | town   coin   lawn |

# Dividing Syllables

1 Label 2 vowels
2 Draw bridge
3 Label C on the bridge
4 Choose Syllable Pattern
5 Split
6 Syllable Type & Label
7 Read or Repeat

# Syllable Type

Say this to remember!

| Rabbits | R | Bossy R |
|---|---|---|
| Eat | E | Magic E |
| Very | V | Vowel Pair |
| Large | L | Consonant-le |
| Orange | O | Open |
| Carrots | C | Closed |

# Letter Types

| VOWELS | CONSONANTS |
|---|---|
| a  e  i  o  u  (y) | Every other letter |

LET'S BREAK WORDS!

# Syllable Patterns

| 1. vc/cv | 2. v/cv | 3. vc/v | 4. v/v | 5. -cle |
|---|---|---|---|---|
| 1st syllable closed | 1st syllable open | 1st syllable closed | 1st syllable open | |
| Jum/bo | Ra/ven | Cab/in | Ne/on | 1st closed: Bot/tle |
| Mag/net | Ro/ver | Rob/ert | Cre/ate | 1st open: No/ble |
| Ship/shape | So/lo | Gav/in | Me/an/der | |

# Thank You

Thank you to From the Pond for the Pond Fonts.
Visit the store on Teachers Pay Teachers.

Thank you to Tracee Orman for the Clip Art Frames.
Visit the store on Teachers Pay Teachers.

Thank you to Creative Clips by Krista Wallden for the great free font!
Visit her store on Teachers Pay Teachers.

Made in the USA
Las Vegas, NV
02 April 2025